LOVE
VS
LIFE

LOVE VS LIFE

Juanee'tah Perry

ARPress
45 Dan Road Suite 5
Canton MA 02021
Hotline: 1(888) 821-0229
Fax: 1(508) 545-7580

Ordering Information:
Quantity sales. Special discounts are available on quantity purchases by corporations, associations, and others. For details, contact the publisher at the address above.

Printed in the United States of America.

ISBN-13:   Paperback   979-8-89356-860-8
                     eBook   979-8-89356-861-5

Library of Congress Control Number: 2024909006

Table of Contents

DEDICATION

I dedicate this book to my kids because I want them to grow up knowing they can do anything they put their mind to. And I pray that life do not take them on the dark road. I also dedicate this book to the people that's in a dark place who are trying to get out. This book is to let them know there is light at the end of the tunnel.

THE BEGINNING

Freshman year in Brown High School Juan was a straight A student. He kept his grades up. He was the captain of the basketball team. All the girls loved themselves some of Juan. Juan really didn't pay attention to the females. All Juan was focused on was his grades and his sport. He wanted to go Pro in basketball one day. Juan finally saw her…. Angel, the girl of his dreams.Juan never really dated anybody he just was used to one-night stands without having any feelings for a female. Angel was a different type of female. Angelalso went to Brown High school. Matter of fact she was a freshman too. So, one day at basketball practice he saw Angel cheerleading and instantly fell in love. They have never said one word to each other ever, but Juan was convinced that they were going to be together. Juan told himself that he was not going to stop until she became his. So, he went up to her after practice andsaid, "Hey girlie what's your name". Angel says, "Hey my name is Angel andI already know your name." Juan says, "Is that so, can I get your number". She says, "I don't know about all that, everytime I turn around there are so many girls that have you on their mind and in their mouths". He tells her ‛you got nothing to worry about them girls means nothing to me I only have eyes for you". Angel looked at him and shook her head. She said, "Let me think about it". And then she walked away. Weeks went by and she has not said a word to Juan. She was playing hard to get until she saw some girl, she did not like talking to him. It was innocent but she did not think that it was.So that night she called Juan out of the blue and said that she will go out withhim. Angel was a very jealous girl. She even was crazy. Juan has only seen the good side so far. This is just the start of their relationship. They started to go on dates. They went to the movies and out to eat. Juan wanted to get to know Angel, so they asked each other questions and talked all night. Juan knew she was the one for him. Juan made it known that he wanted Angel to be with him for a very long time and he will do anything to keep her. Every week Juan took her out and eventually he found out her favorite places to go and favorite things to do so he started taking her to all these places. It's been only a few months and they were falling in love with each other. Angel just knew she found the one, or she thought she did.

From Highschool to college Juan had his eyes on Angel and he was not letting that go. Juan knew who he wanted, and he made it very clear. Angel loved herself some Juan. They always were happy in public, but nobody knewwhat went on behind closed doors. At home where Angel and Juan lived together Juan took control. Juan was the man of the house, and he swore that since he is the man of the house that he has all rights to be in control. Angel was miserable but she didn't want to show Juan that. Angel kept all her feelings inside bottled up. She didn't know how bad it could get if she kept all her feelings bottled up. So, two years went by, and Juan and Angel are still together. Mind you Angel has not mentioned to her family about what happens in her relationship. Her family loved themselves some Juan. They looked at him like he was her soul mate. Angel knew if she did not become happy with Juan, she was going to do something drastic. Angel asked Juan "Do you love me". Juan says, "of course I do, why do you ask". She said, "Because you treat me so crazy like you control everything I do". He said, "well I want the best for you, so I am trying to make that happen for you".She says "I understand that I really do but you are really doing too much. I need you to calm down for me". Juan did not say anything after that he just nod at her and looked away. He walked outside and then walked back inside in silence. He then balled up his fist and punched her in the face and said "bitch, you are my girl I can do whatever I want in this house and to you.Do not ever tell me what I am doing wrong. Things can get worse if you keepquestioning me, Now I love you with everything in me and I get real mad when the love of my life is questioning how I love her. Baby, now I am sorry for hitting you and I'll never do it again". Angel eye is black and blue at this point. She did not even shed a tear. All she did was say okay. Angel stillloved Juan. This was the first time he ever hit her, so she prays he never hither again. So, she wore dark sunglasses for about a week, and she also stayed in the house. She did not want to go anywhere for people to see. She did not tell anybody what had happened. She just knew a change was bound to happen she just didn't know what it was just yet.

Juan and Angel have been together for two years. Angel was not happy, and Juan knew she wasn't, but he didn't care if she was happy or not. Juan only cared about him. His method is if she leaves or even thinks about leaving her life is going to end. One day Angel made herself a social media account. Well, a private one so Juan didn't find out. She starts talking to a man named John on the social media account. She told John that she is in a relationship, but she can have friends. She told him that she can only talk on social media because her boyfriend is crazy.

Four years now and they are still together. It's been very rocky, but they are still trying to make it work. What Angel does not know is that her friend John has been watching her every move.

Juan continued to still be controlling but that's just who he is. Angel figured one day he will change his ways to where they can do things together. That's not ever going to happen. Juan says it all the time, can't nobody change him not even Angel can change him.

So, Angel went for a ride by herself, she sees a black car following her so now she is scared. Everywhere she turned so did the black car. Now she's speeding down a street and what do you know the black car starts speeding too. The black car is turning the same way she turns, so she stops all of a sudden and so did the black car. Now the creepy part is that she never saw John a day in her life so how did he know who she was and what she looked like. Her social media account doesn't have a picture on there. So, she got out of the car and there he was all light skin and muscular with a big grin on his face. He says "Hi Angel I'm John and I just had to see you. She says, "umhow did you find me, how did you know what car I drive, how did you know what I looked like, who are you and what do you want from me." He says "I did my research; we have been talking online for two years and we haven't seen each other at all. So, I took it upon myself to come find you. I have been following you around for over a year. I see how your man is treating you, I'mhere to tell you that I will treat you so much better. I know you got a man, so we don't have to tell him". She says to him "that is a bunch of bullshit, and I will have to think about that. My man is really crazy and if he finds out that I am talking to you or any guy for that matter, he will kill me and you together". He says, "I don't think that will happen, just think about it and then hit me up". He then walked away, got into his car and sped off.

So, now Angel gets back in her car and she's scared out her mind. Like did that just happen? Did her internet dude just come out of nowhere? Did her dude set that up? Now she got a lot going on in her head. She drives home and takes a bath and goes straight to sleep.

The next day Juan is being such a gentleman towards Angel. He is loving her and being there for her all throughout the day. For some odd reason Angel woke up in sweat. Now Juan is trying to figure out why she got sick within twenty-four hours. Angel just wants to know why and how John found her. Who does John know? Throughout the day Angel was in the days. She was not focused at all. But Juan was very smart, and he just knew something was way off with Angel. He asked her "is you okay babes you seem a little off today". She says, "I am okay just not feeling well". So, they both enjoyed the rest of the day together.

As the days, weeks, and months go by Angel has been hanging around John when she can because she did not want Juan to know that she was talking to someone else. So, John has been asking Angel if he can take her out instead of just seeing her for two hours here and there. She keeps telling him no because something bad might happen that she did not want to happen. She keeps laughing at him like he is really trying to ruin her life. Her boyfriend is beyond crazy, but John does not care about that, and he makes that very clear everyday. John made it his duty that he is going to get her if it is the last thing he does.

So, one day there was a family gathering at Juan's father's house. He feels he can bring Angel to finally meet his family. So, they go to his father's house where there is a bunch of laughter and love all around until Juan's brother comes to the house. When Angel saw John and realized that John was Juan's brother, she automatically got sick to her stomach. She told Juan that she wants to go home. Juan asked her, "Angel are you okay"? Angel said, "Yes I am fine I just want to go home I do not feel good". He says, "okay we can go home". So, Juan takes Angel home, in the car she did not say a word she was just confused. She knew that she had to stop talking to John because Juan and John are brothers. So, when John texts her asking if he can see her, she says that she can't ever be around him again. She was so mad that he did not tell her that he was Juan's brother. She says "John you ought to be ashamed of yourself. I told you, personal things about me and my boyfriend and you pretended like you care. You don't care about my life or yours, because I guarantee you that if he was to find out I was talking to you me, and you both would be dead". John says, "I know I should have told you that Juan was my brother but if I told you that then you wouldn't even have given me a chance". Angel told him to not ever call her again.

John was no fool and he was not about to fall back from Angel at all. He told himself that whatever it takes he was going to get Angel whether she likes it or not. Angel doesn't know what is about to happen, especially dealing with John knowing he is Juan's brother. John thought that he was the man, that he was untouchable. Well, Angel has been trying to stay away from John for 6 months now. But it seems like wherever she wants she sees him or someone that looks like him. Angel felt like she was living in a twilight zone. Everytime Angel closed her eyes there was John's face. So now Angel is losing her mind because she doesn't know what to do or how to get away from John. She just wants to forget about him. Well, little did she know things were about to get rocky. She felt like she should just go for a ride to clear her mind. She gets in her car and once again, a black car is following behind her. But this time she wasn't going down without a fight. So, she stopped her car and so did the black car. When John got out of the car, he had rage in his eyes. Angel saw that rage but, she told herself that she will not let him scare her. So, John says "hi Angel did you miss me"? She just shook her head No. But all John did was laugh while walking towards her and unzipping his pants. He grabs her by her neck very rough to the point she couldn't breathe. He then unzipped her pants and pulled them down. Now, mind you she can't breathe which means she can't scream. He sticks his dick inside her and start fucking her really hard while he still has his hands around her neck. He did cum in her, but he did not stop until he was ready to stop. He threw her on the ground and kicked her. He then got into his car and sped off while she was on the ground crying in fear. Angel finally got up and went back into her car and she is crying in disgust and in pain. Angel is trying to get herself together before she goes home to her boyfriend. She just knows once Juan finds out what happened he is going to be so angry with so much rage. There is no telling what is about to happen.

So, this is where it all begins.

So, I'm going to tell you how I died. I'm going to tell you from the beginning to the end. My name is Angel and I am currently not living anymore. So, after John raped me that night, I was so scared to go home to my boyfriend. Juan is so insane. So, the next day everything was going fine until my stomach started feeling really weird to the point I started throwing up. I just thought I had the stomach flu, so I didn't even bother going to the hospital. I got in the shower thinking I would feel a lot better after. Juan is looking at me like I'm crazy. He had a concerned look on his face. He asks me "Baby are you okay". I assured him that I was fine. Did I think Juan was okay with that answer, No I did not. I knew Juan was not okay with how he was looking at me. He is very smart but crazy at the same time. I loved me some Juan but not when he is mad I don't. When Juan is mad, I just know my day is going to be bad already.

Anyways I thought I just had the stomach flu or something. But a week went by and I was still feeling sick and I was still throwing up. I just knew at this point something wasn't right. So, Juan took me to the hospital and guess what, I found out I was pregnant. Now, mind you Juan still don't know about John and what had happened. So, when Juan found out I was pregnant he was so happy and I didn't want to take that away from him so I basically made it seem as if the baby was his. It's just that I had never seen him so happy in my life. While I'm pregnant he was such a gentleman. All throughout my pregnancy I prayed for the baby to come out looking like me. Juan went to every doctor's appointment with me. It was like a dream come true. I always wanted him to treat me like a princess. I was thinking maybe I should be pregnant more often if this is the life I am going to be living.

So now I'm five months pregnant and it's time to find out the sex of the baby. This is the day me and Juan have been waiting for. So, we go into the room and the doctor is doing the sonogram and she says, "congrats parents' you guys are having a precious baby girl". At that point hearing those words I just knew that I cannot ever let that monster John to ever come near my daughter. I just knew I had to change my ways. Everything I do I do for her.

As the weeks go by, we have to pick out baby names. Since I have been doing so much trying to get ready to bring my baby into the world, I had told Juan that he can name the baby. Saying those words made him the happiest man ever. So, while I was stressing to get everything ready for my daughter Juan was stressing to find out a baby girl's name. It's almost time for the baby to come at this point. Juan has a name for the baby finally.

It's baby time now. We are finally welcoming Sahara Myrical Rivera. And what do you know she came out looking exactly like me, so I know things are about to be great with my little family. Juan signed the birth certificate, so I know it's real. We were in this hospital for three days and now it's time to take our baby girl home. All I can think about is if John is going to try something crazy. I have a daughter now so I'm a much different person. I will go above and beyond for my baby. We are finally home now and Juan has not put the baby down not once. I just know Sahara is going to love her daddy.

The next morning after we brought Sahara home, I woke up and the house was decorated with roses. I'm amazed right now because I just know Juan did all this while I was asleep. I walked in the kitchen and he is on one knee with a diamond ring. He finally said the magic words I've been dying to hear since high school. "Will you marry me Angel". I shed a tear and said "yes". I could cry right now. I'm really about to marry my best friend. I just knew Juan was my soul mate. I do know one day I am going to have to tell him what happened with John. But to be honest I never did anything serious with John except for him raping me which will be on him once Juan finds out. In the meantime, me and Juan will be living our best life with our daughter.

So, one year went by, our daughter is one years old now and we are finally married after so many years of being together. People used to always tell me once you have a kid with someone everything changes. Well, in my case I think everything had changed for the better.

Well, that's what I thought. I worked in the mornings and Juan worked at night. We were so overwhelmed, but we made a promise that we are going to work it all out together. Not realizing that we both were tired, our daughter is our world, so we just did not give up no matter what. Well, we did not give up on her but at this point I was starting to feel neglected from Juan. I was feeling that Juan was giving up on us. So, since I had become a mom, my eyes have been wide open. I know he works at night, but I know damn well he don't work overnight so with him coming home early in the mornings I just know something is not right. So, one night when Juan went to work, I decided that me and Sahara are going to go out for a ride. We went past Juan's job and that's when I saw her. A Caucasian female with blonde hair and blue eyes. I just knew something had to be done. The things that were going on in my head were ridiculous. I am so mad that I want to fight but I refused to let my daughter see me get mad. So as the days go by, I did not tell Juan that I knew about that girl. Shit, I did some things that I know Juan would not be happy about. So, I figured that I will just take matters in my own hands.

Now, this is the moment that my life turned for the worst. So, it's Juan's off day and he's asleep with Sahara. So, I sneak out of the house, so I don't wake him up. I'm dressed in all black with gloves on that won't show any fingerprints if there is any. Now, mind you I have to do this the smart way. I have an extra change of clothes. I drive up to the job. My mind is filled with so much. I pulled a mask over my face and went into the job and snatched that blonde hair female that I saw talking to my husband and I stabbed her a million times and then I shot her three times in her heart. I had the silencer on so nobody could hear it so I left her body there. I got back in the car and changed my clothes. I got rid of the clothes that I had on so it wouldn't ever be found. I had to burn the clothes. I had to burn the clothes. I then went back home and they are still asleep so I sneaked back in the bed and I went to sleep. The next morning, I kissed Juan and told him I will see him later after work. So, after that I did not think about what I did. I just know when I became a mom, I made a promise that I will make sure my family stays together even if I have to do something drastic. So, since then Juan has been coming home from work on time. He has not said anything to me about how his days have been at work. I just knew I was untouchable at that point. I loved my little family and I will do anything to keep them together. Sahara loves daddy and if anything, ever tries to get in the middle of that I will go crazy. My daughter deserves the world.

Sahara just turned three years old and we figure it's time she meets her family. So, we have a get together at Juan's dad house so his family can meet her. I just knew this was a bad idea. We all had a good time until John showed up. Like who the fuck invited him. I just know he is going to piss me off. The way my mind has been going lately he really does not want to start with me. So, I'm in the kitchen making my daughter a plate to eat and the man John comes in and tells me that he knows my daughter is his. I told him that she is not and never will be his. He keeps staring at my baby, I'm like stop looking at her and please stay away from her. So, I let her enjoy the rest of her day and then we went home and got ready for bed.

So now that she is three, she is able to go to preschool. So, it's her first day of school and she just was not feeling it at all. The teacher told me that she sat in the corner by herself but when she is at home, she's a whole different person. She's very active at home. I really did not understand why she was such a loner at school. So, when I picked her up from school that day, I took her out to eat and to just have a chat with her. While we were talking, she told me she didn't like school and she wanted to stay home with us. I had to explain to her that mommy and daddy work now that she's in school so then when she comes home, she can be home with us the rest of the day. It made her feel better a little bit. So, I told her to let start again tomorrow with school. As I look at my daughter, I see me all in her. I just want her life to be better than mine. So, another year goes by and here Juan goes again staying out all night again. He tells me he has been hanging with his boys after work, but I was not believing that at all. So, when I dropped Sahara off to school I just so happened to ride by his job. And what do you know he was not there. So now I want to know where he at, because why aren't you at work where you're supposed to be. Now I'm at my breaking point but I still try to stay calm and collected. So instead of waiting for him to get to work I just went on to work since I still have a child I have to provide for. So, when I got home, he still was not at home. So now I'm fuming because he been M.I.A. all day. Why at one in the morning he comes stumbling in the house drunk as a skunk. He is looking at me with rage, but I look at him like he lost his mind. He walks in Sahara's room to make sure she was asleep and then comes back in the room where I was and sat next to me in silence. So, he looks at me and asks me what I have been doing. I told him I haven't been doing anything. He then looks at me and says, "I know what you did". So now my heart is pounding, like how did he find out. He looked at me and cried, "why did you do that to her". So, I told him "because I see you talking to her so I got angry". We are supposed to be married with a baby and he is out here talking to females. He looked at me and said, "what are you so angry for she was just a coworker like she did not deserve that". "I really been staying overnight at work. But you wouldn't know that because you barely talk to me". So, now I'm mad at myself at this point. I really killed that girl for no reason. So now I'm ready for him to tell me he wants a divorce, but he did not say that. Instead, he shook his head and went to sleep with his daughter. He told me that I need to take a breather and I did just that. I went into the room and went to sleep. I'm still trying to figure out who seen me do that.

Anyways, the next day I tried to talk to him and he just gave me the silent treatment. The whole week I wanted him to hold me. He wouldn't even hold me. Better yet he didn't sleep in the room with me at all. Everytime he looked at me it was like he didn't even want to see me ever again. A week went by before he said something to me. He looked at me and said, "why are you so crazy, this is not the girl I fell in love with back in high school". I never thought he would be this mad at me. I love me some Juan, but he was not happy with me. My daughter is four years old and very anti-social. I wonder if I'm the reason why she acts like that. I do know she watches my every move, but I try to be the best mom I can but it's hard when I have things rolling around in my head. I feel like a failure as a wife and a mother. Months went by and now my daughter is turning five years old. Juan is still mad at me, but he will be fine.

So now that Sahara is five years old, she's been becoming more antisocial in public. Around this time there was little kids gone missing, and most of these children goes to Sahara's school. Now my mind wasn't where it was supposed to be. I should have just been more focused on Sahara than on my marriage. Now, she may have been five years old, but she was very smart. I don't know what's going on in her little head of hers, but she's been killing these kids and burying them. Now, if I wanted to I could of turned her in but, then they would of looked at me and her dad and I wasn't having that. So, I just didn't say anything about what I know I just kept trying to figure out why was my child behavior so horrifying. I love my daughter and I thought I was doing everything right. I guess it's true when they say that kids watch your every move. I know I may not be perfect, but I really have been trying to hide my actions. I done did some crazy things, but I didn't think my five-year-old daughter would do what I do.

Let's not get on my daughter's behavior when the man John is still stalking my life. He keeps making threats and all. And to be honest I don't know why he keeps trying my patience. They don't call me toxic for no reason. When I set my mind on something I gets it done. So, with him keep threatening me it's just going to make me do something that I most likely won't regret. See when I started talking to him it was only because Juan wasn't showing me any attention. But then I knew John was crazy when he said he knew who I was from day one. But it put the icing on the cake when I found out that him and Juan was brothers. Then he put a trigger in my back when he called himself raping me. Now that I have Sahara the man has been harassing me because he knows that she is really his. But I still refuse to tell Juan about what happened that night so I'm going to handle it myself. When I get a chance away from Juan without him wondering where I'm going, I'm going to make it to where John don't ever see the light of day. So, either I put him behind bars, or I just take his life. This man swears he knows me, but he just doesn't know what is about to happen to him. John really will get himself hurt messing with me. He's playing a game that I love to play. So, I go and still be the mother that I know to be to my daughter. I love being a mother, but I feel like I'm failing as a mother because of how she has been acting out lately.

Here comes John stalking me again. I had just dropped my daughter off at school and I saw his car approaching mine. So, I stopped my car because now I'm ready to play this game and I'm going to play it right. John is about to feel my wrath. He gets out of the car in rage. When I saw his face, I just knew he was mad. So, he says to me "I am going to kill you Angel and I mean like really kill you". I looked at him and laughed "yeah okay, not if I don't kill you first". So, he says, "you're really going to take me from my child before you even introduce me to her". I go to my car and grab my gun and my gloves. I put my gloves on and cocked my gun back and said "John you will never meet my daughter ever in life again. She will never know who you are". I was so mad and angry at him, and I just wanted him gone. I shot John multiple times in the chest until he was limp and there was no breath left in his body. Now that John is finally gone, I can live my life freely.

As the years went by things did not go as smoothly as I wanted them to. My daughter has been acting real crazy lately. She's been staying to herself, but she also been lashing out on people for who knows what reason. So, you know it's her tenth birthday now and she has been having really bad seizures. Who would of thought on her tenth birthday it would be ruined by a really bad seizure that leads her to the hospital. Now I had to work this day, so I didn't know what was going on. I do know the doctor asked Juan to give up some blood for his daughter. Now in my head I didn't think anything was going to happen. I didn't think that they were going to happen. I didn't think that they were going to have to give her any blood. I also didn't think that Juan's blood wasn't going to match hers because Juan and John were brothers, they should have had the same type of blood. Well, that was not the case when the doctor seen that Juan's blood did not match Sahara's they told him that he wasn't really her father, which I just knew he was crushed on the inside of his soul. I went home from work and all I can see is Juan sitting on the couch with rage in his eyes. He looks at me and says, "so the doctors told me I wasn't Sahara's father". I looked at him and cried "I wanted to tell you so bad, but I was scared, your brother John raped me and then that's when I found myself pregnant. I knew you would be a great father and a wonderful husband, so I didn't say anything about it. I also knew if I would have told you, you would have been fuming with rage". He then says "why you didn't come to me, we were supposed to be a team. I would have confronted John I have not spoken to him in some years". With tears running down my face I looked at him and congested "I killed him some years ago. He kept stalking me and trying to come near my daughter and I wasn't having it". He then looks at me and gives me a hug. When I looked in his eyes, I just knew he meant every word when he said that he loved me when we got married. He told me he will stick by me no matter what. Now when I killed John, I hid his body really well by throwing it in the ocean. They found his body but there was nothing pointing it to me. When I do something, I make sure I do it and I finish it. My daughter Sahara was eavesdropping when me and Juan were speaking. She now knows that Juan was not her biological father, and I killed the man that was. I didn't think life would get like this, but I guess everything happens for a reason. So, the next morning I offered to take Sahara to school. She says to me "I know what you did". I looked at her and said, "I know and I'm sorry for everything I was just trying to protect you". She looks at me with tears and says, "mommy I love you I always will but I'm going to give you a taste of your own medicine". Now I didn't know what she meant by that until she went in the kitchen and grabbed a steak knife and ran right to me and stabbed me and didn't stop. Now I just knew she was angry and to be honest the death of me will bite her right in the ass. I just know I'm going to come back for her, but does she know that.

THIS IS NOT THE END

The two couple was so in love. Matter fact they were high school sweethearts. Nobody saw this coming. Angel was such a sweetheart until she really started to get physically abused by Juan in the beginning. She didn't care about the abuse, she just wanted what was hers and that's Juan. Well, that's where her mentality was. Angel seemed innocent but she's not. She was a very jealous girl but not in Juan's eyes Juan used to look at her like she was the only girl in the world. He was in love with Angel so much he did not understand the actions that she did. Now that she's gone, he doesn't even know what to do or how to react. He even knows the things he did to her wasn't right but to be honest when he hit her once he never really hit her again. Now everytime he looks at Sahara he sees Angel. He made it his duty to not give up on Sahara. He knows what she did, but he figures that she is going to feel the pain. She has to carry that with her for the rest of her life. Juan says he is going to take one day at a time. He is still Sahara's father; he is all she knows. Now he bit his tongue at this point because Sahara is still out of control. He doesn't know what to do with her, but he thinks maybe it's just how she's grieving. She is talking to boys which Juan is not going for. But when he says stuff that he doesn't like she'll get mad and screams "you're not my dad and you can't tell me what to do". But when she gets to the point where she knows that she has nobody she goes right to him. He knows Sahara loves him, she just grieving, and she feels she can do whatever she wants to. He is still going to be there for her whenever she needs him. Juan has been watching Sahara's actions and it's been really scary lately. Life still goes on.

MOMMY'S BACK

Nobody believes me when I say that I feel it in my soul that I know my mom is coming for me. I'm eighteen years old now and everywhere I go I see her. Now my body is shaking with fear because I killed my mother and that was so wrong. I do miss my mom with everything in me, but I know life is never going to be the same. My mom definitely held it down even though I gave her a run for her money. I just can't believe I killed my own mom because I was angry. I was ten years old but that doesn't really justify my actions. Now I'm walking around looking all crazy, I can barely think straight, nor can I eat right. When I close my eyes, I see her. One night I was just lying in my bed staring at the wall until I seen her. She looked at me and said, "are you happy to see me did you miss me, it's been a long time". I shed some tears. I had no words at this point. I just knew this was one of the things that would make me lose my mind. I said, "I'm sorry mommy I really am". I done got on my knees and I started praying and begging for my life. She started laughing at me, she said "God don't have nothing to do with this". I just kept crying and screaming until my dad Juan busted through the door because my cries woke him up. But do you guys know when he came in the room she disappeared. Now I', scared at this point. He says, "what's wrong what happened". I started pointing to where she was standing at and started screaming, "mommy's here she's back, she's really back, she's coming for me". He looked at me and I just knew he felt sorry for me. He cried with me. He kept saying things was going to be okay, but I knew deep down it wasn't. Life is really getting the best of me at this point. I'm a girl and I need my mom but not in this way. I messed up really badly. I killed the only one that loved me till the end of time. Now my mind is all over the place. I feel like I can't do everything. I just can't believe I killed my own mother not realizing how much I really need her. Now I'm being hunted by my dead mother. I swear this can't be life right now. My mind is going crazy. My dad doesn't even look at me no more.

So why was I in class and here she goes again out the window of my classroom looking at me. Now I'm in my senior year in high school and I'm as scared as ever at this very moment. So, at this point I asked the teacher if I can be excused, I'm not feeling well and she says I can. Now I know she seen my face. She just didn't say anything, I went to the bathroom and there she goes. I then asked her what she is doing there. She says, "what do you mean I'm here to take you back with me it's time to go". I started crying instantly "I am so sorry for what I did to you, but I am not going anywhere no time soon". So, she disappears, and the teacher walks in on me sitting on the bathroom floor shaking and with tears in my eyes, when I mentioned to the teacher that I keep seeing my dead mother and that she's actually been talking to me. She looked at me and shed a tear for me. She calls my dad and tells him what happened and because I'm going insane, he admits me into Brown Mental Hospital. He says he is only doing this to help, and I couldn't do anything but do what he says, in order for my sanity to come back.

Sitting in this padded white room all by myself just thinking about life is just scaring me all over again. But I guess being in this room gives me peace but I'm still seeing her wherever I go to sleep and when I wake up in the morning. But I guess that's what my life is going to be like because of what I have done. But to keep my mind off of things there's this doctor that is so fine and his name is Sebastian. He is light skin with long straight hair. One of the things I like. I may not know him, but I know I'm going to find out. My dad done lost his mind putting me in here with this cute ass doctor. So, Sebastian comes in and I'm in the days. When he started talking, I fell in love instantly with his Spanish accent. I asked him his name and then he asked me mine. When I told him my name, I just knew he was going to be mine. I didn't even care that I was in the mental part of the hospital I had to have him. He may not have known it yet, but he is definitely my dude. The man comes in my room everyday until this one day a different doctor came in, but he kept apologizing to me saying that he is sorry that a doctor hasn't been to see me. I then told him a doctor named Sebastian been to see me everyday. The doctor says that there is no doctor named Sebastian that works in this hospital. So, when he said that I instantly got scared. So, he goes out and says he will be back later. Now I'm scared because if he is not a doctor then who is he and where did he come from. So, the next day the man Sebastian comes in and now I'm fuming because how does he know me. So, I finally asked him "who are you. I found out that you are not a doctor here at all". He started laughing "I'm not a doctor at all it took you a long time to figure it out but to be honest I know all about you, I know you killed your mother when you were ten. I have actually been following you around for some years now and to be honest you are really crazy, and we will never work out, actually I'm going to be the one to give you a taste of your own medicine". I can't believe I even had a crush on him. I now know he doesn't even care he wants me dead like a lot of people do. I can't really be mad right now because I done did some stuff that I shouldn't have. I know consequences have to happen. So, before I get myself killed, I know what I have to do. I called my dad and told him to come get me and that's exactly what he did. When he came to get me, I told him to take me to my mom's grave and then to the prison. At my mom's grave I apologized for everything I did to her. I even told her how much I needed her and that I loved her and missed her so much. I even told her my next move, that I will be turning myself in well at least I'm going to try to. So now I asked my dad to take me to the prison so I can turn myself in. When I said that my dad says he is not doing that. He says that he signed me up for college that I have been accepted to and didn't even know. So, I guess I'm going to college to become a doctor, a real doctor at that. I thanked my dad for everything. I thought life was going to end but I guess God has a different plan for me, he's giving me a second chance and to be honest that is all I need. I'm going to prove it to myself that I can change. My life will change, and I promise you this is not the end.